A CENTURY *of*
BELFAST

The floor of Combe Barbour's Falls Foundry in North Howard Street, off the Falls Road, one of the most important of Belfast's engineering industries. Begun in 1845 by James Combe, one of a number of Scots who contributed to Belfast's nineteenth-century industrial development, it specialised in manufacturing machinery for the spinning and weaving processes in the linen industry. Inventions from the 1820s and 1830s which enabled textiles to be mass-produced in factories required resourceful engineering skills which the business could provide. It also specialised in quadruple-expansion engines for export to cotton mills in India. It was one of the first businesses to have electric light introduce to assist its production.

A CENTURY *of* BELFAST

TREVOR PARKHILL &
VIVIENNE POLLOCK

National
Museums
Northern
Ireland

The
History
Press

First published in 2001 by Sutton Publishing Limited

This edition first published in 2010 by
The History Press
The Mill, Brimscombe Port,
Stroud, Gloucestershire, GL5 2QG
www.thehistorypress.co.uk

Reprinted 2011

British Library Cataloguing in Publication Data
A catalogue record for this book is available from the British Library.

ISBN 978 0 7509 5012 1

Illustrations

Front endpaper: This panoramic view of the Abercorn basin and, on the other side of
the river, the Belfast docks stretching to the distance shows the launch of the Coast
Line passenger/cargo vessel *Leinster* on 20 May 1945 from Harland & Wolff's Abercorn
Yard. The *Leinster* and her sister ship, the *Munster*, were two of the many large vessels
commissioned from the Belfast shipyard as the Second World war drew to a close.
Back endpaper: Photographed as the days began to stretch in the first summer of the
new millennium, this image of a traffic-free Royal Avenue recalls much earlier days of
leisurely, car-free shopping and sight-seeing.
Half-title page: Two Belfasts for the price of one. The RAF plane, 'Belfast', built by local aircraft
manufacturers Short Bros & Harland, flying over its native city, with the City Hall neatly
tucked under its port wing and Divis and Black Mountains in the background.
Title page: This wonderfully framed photograph shows the inside of the gate of the Belfast
Poor House (the metal-wrought letters read 'Belfast Charitable Society') and the view down
Frederick Street to the city centre in the days when hand-carts were still a common means
of conveyance on Belfast's streets.

Typeset in 11/14pt Photina
Typesetting and origination by
Sutton Publishing Limited.
Printed and bound in England.

Contents

Entrance official J.A.W. Wilberforce stands proudly outside his richly decorated ticket-house to welcome visitors to the 'Coronation' Show at the Royal Ulster Agriculture Society's grounds at Balmoral on 29 May 1937.

Introduction

In 1900 Belfast was the fastest-growing city in the British Isles. During the preceding century, its population had mushroomed from that of a sizeable market town of c. 20,000 to a thriving industrial city of 350,000, making it the twelfth largest city in the United Kingdom and, for the first time, bigger than Dublin. Its magnetism was such that it had nearly trebled in size in the forty years since 1860; moreover, in 1900 only one-fifth of the people living there had been born in the town, the rest being recent migrants attracted by the range of employment opportunities it offered. Unlike most other industrial cities in Britain, only a handful of the arrivals were from abroad: by 1914 there was an Italian and a Jewish community, the latter numbering only 1,200.

Belfast had only been incorporated as a city as late as 1888, a status symbolised in 1906 by the construction of the city hall. This imposing building replaced the White Linen Hall which had served as the centre of the linen trade throughout the nineteenth century. The mechanisation of the spinning and weaving processes in the linen industry had been an integral part of Belfast's nineteenth-century industrialisation. In the years to 1914, the city's power-weaving factories produced the great bulk of linen cloth, particularly fine damask.

Shipbuilding, particularly of large passenger liners, proved to be the backbone of the city's industrial prowess. The dawning of 1900 had seen Harland & Wolff just launch four ships for the White Star Line, including *Oceanic II*, then the largest ship afloat. The apogee of Belfast's industrial achievement might be identified as having taken place on 31 May 1911, when the RMS *Titanic* was launched at the Harland & Wolff yard. By 1914, the two yards, Harland & Wolff and Workman Clark, had become as the most productive shipbuilders in Britain.

Linen and shipbuilding also generated business for a range of service industries which contributed to the vigour of the city's economic well-being. This was perhaps most evident in rope-making. Ships and ship-building created a demand for heavy ropes which was met by the Belfast Rope Works Co. Managed by Samuel Smiles, it employed up to 3,000 before the First World War. Belfast also had one of the largest tobacco factories (Gallaher's) in the world. Both commodities were exported on a large scale.

Other industries included the production of alcoholic and non-alcoholic drinks. Belfast firms were responsible for well over half the total whiskey exports from Ireland and a dozen firms produced 'aerated waters': Ross's claimed to have invented the gin and tonic as a way of marketing their tonic water with quinine. Among the city's several notable engineering firms, there were three car manufacturers which, by 1913, had built over 150 models of this revolutionary form of transport.

This generally rosy picture of prosperity continued more or less unabated throughout the First World War. The two Belfast shipyards led the response to the

The *Titanic* in Belfast Lough, 2 April 1912. Thirteen days later she sank in the north-west Atlantic with the loss of nearly 1,500 lives.

shipping losses incurred at the hands of the German U-boats and between them launched over 660,000 tons of destroyers, cruisers and hospital ships as well as patrol boats and cargo carriers, providing employment for 29,000. However, the postwar world-wide slump, two of whose main casualties were shipbuilding and textile production, would, from 1921, bring serious reversal to this progress.

By 2000 the name 'Belfast' would become synonymous with the generation of civil and political unrest popularly known as 'The Troubles'. In fact there had been serious community disturbances in the city throughout the nineteenth century. In spite of its industrial burgeoning evident in the early 1900s, there had also been sown by then the seeds of the violence that would be beamed to the world's television screens from the late 1960s.

The increasingly bitter tensions between those in favour of keeping the union with Britain and those who favoured a form of independence for Ireland came to a head on 12 September 1912, Covenant Day, when 250,000 gathered at the City Hall to express their opposition to legislation granting Ireland Home Rule from the Westminster Parliament. The day of reckoning, postponed by the onset of war in 1914, returned to the city in the summer of 1920. For the next two years Belfast found itself embroiled in a series of incidents associated with the Partition of Ireland and the establishment of Northern Ireland, during which some 500 people were killed.

From that time Belfast became the capital of the new Northern Ireland state, a position signified in 1933 by the opening of the newly built Parliament Buildings at Stormont in east Belfast. Its grandeur jarred with the number of houses built by the corporation in the interwar years: 16 by direct contract and 2,600 subsidised. The city's economic trough, begun in the early 1920s, deepened after 1929 and continued throughout the 1930s. Among the serious losses to the economy was the liquidation in 1935 of Workman Clark, know locally as 'the wee yard' though twice earlier in the century it had produced more in one year than any other shipyard in the world.

Unemployment, which at times amounted to more than 50,000 people, over a quarter of the working population, ensured that social privation was endemic in the interwar period. It was famously exemplified by the October 1932 Outdoor Relief Strike, remembered for being one of the few times when Protestant Shankill Road and Catholic Falls Road laid aside their differences to unite in a protest march to the gates of the Union workhouse (later the site of the City Hospital). An indication of the poverty evident in the city is that over 50 per cent of all deaths under fifteen years of age were caused by infectious diseases. Of these tuberculosis – an accepted barometer of malnutrition – accounted for half of all deaths in the 15–25 age range and was by far the most dangerous.

A measure of prosperity bolstered the city during the Second World War with the revival of its principal manufactories – shipbuilding and textiles – which contributed to Britain's war effort. The commonly accepted view that Belfast was too far from Germany to be threatened by air raids was shattered in April 1941 when over 900 were killed, more during one night's raid than in any other British city outside London. Nearly 200 were killed in a subsequent raid on the city the following month. Overall, some 3,000 houses in the city were destroyed and many more damaged. The longer-term postwar regeneration was similar to that of other bombed cities. By the early 1950s Belfast began to see its hospitals modernised and more secondary schools and public housing estates built.

The linen industry in the years immediately after the war regained some of the ground lost earlier in the century and tried to modernise. By 1952, however, the world-wide reduction in orders affected the city to the extent that over 10,000 of its linen workers were unemployed. Thereafter the competition of acrylic fibres led to the closure of the best-known names in the Belfast textile industry, the York Street Flax Spinning Company, Broadway Damask Co. and the Brookfield Spinning Co. among them.

Although employment in the shipbuilding industry did not regain the heights of pre-First World War days, the relative progress that was maintained throughout the 1950s was capped by the launch in 1961 of the large passenger liner, *Canberra*. Thereafter, Harland & Wolff made losses every year from 1964 and the decline has continued since then: the Harland & Wolff shipyard at the close of the twentieth century bore little relation to the picture a hundred years earlier.

Boundary and other changes have seen the city's population change significantly over the last hundred years, indeed dramatically in the final quarter of a century. The estimated population in 2000, 286,000, was almost 25 per cent less than it had been in 1971 (416,679). One of the most striking demographic features has been the alterations in the religious composition of the city's population. In 1901 one quarter of the population was Catholic; by 1991 this percentage had grown to something approaching 50 per cent.

Donegall Place and, beyond it, Royal Avenue, viewed from the top of the City Hall at any time from 1970 until the late 1990s. The 'normality' of the scene lies in the security barrier entrance through which the buses are passing. All other traffic was banned from this city centre thoroughfare, but could travel along the front of the City Hall. Indeed, the pedestrianisation of the city centre proved to be a benefit that continues to be enforced.

Mary Peters (later Dame Mary) returns to Belfast displaying the gold medal she had just won in the Ladies' Pentathlon at the 1972 Olympic Games in Munich.

The community tensions that have been brought to a head in mixed areas have led to significant and often precipitous local shifts of population, particularly since 1969. The televisual image of Belfast on screens throughout the world has tended to ignore the extensive efforts at building better relations between communities in what has been a bitterly divided society. The work of the Community Relations Council with community groups, and the inauguration in Belfast in the 1980s of an integrated schools movement – attended by Catholic and Protestant children – which has spread throughout Northern Ireland, have gone some way to creating better understanding at community level.

The city's absorption with the sporting achievements of local heroes characterised the warm welcomes given to Mary Peters on her return to the city in 1972 with the gold medal she won at the Munich Olympics. Equal pride was generated by the award in 1995 of the Nobel Prize for Literature to Seamus Heaney who, while

Belfast City Hall,
Christmas 1938.

a lecturer in the department of English at The Queen's University, had played a prominent role in the city's remarkable literary flowering since the late 1960s.

The scars on the cityscape and on the inhabitants' collective psyche that have resulted from what *The Times* of London has called the 'suppressed civil war' since the late 1960s are confirmed by the grim statistics. Of the 3,376 people killed in Northern Ireland during the Troubles, almost exactly a half (1,647) have died in the city of Belfast. The great majority of explosions and other recorded terrorist incidents have also taken place there. The relentless terrorist bombing campaign and the security measures taken to counteract it may be thought to have been single-handedly responsible for the radical changes in the urban landscape of the city over the last thirty years. However, far-reaching renovations and urban development, including shopping centres such as Castle Court, stylish Housing Executive public housing and, more recently, purpose-built town house and apartment developments have equally played their part in the striking renewal apparent throughout the 1990s. This *fin de siècle* blossoming is personified, as it were, in the construction of the Waterfront Hall and the Odyssey Arena which symbolise the spirit of renewal that has recently characterised the city.

In the midst of these thorough-going changes, it is perhaps worth noting that the city remains one of the most picturesquely situated in the British Isles. In 1900 it nestled, by 2000 it sprawled, between the Belfast Lough and the Craigantlet Hills to the south and east, and, to the north and west, the Cave Hill, an impressive landmark which gives the city one of its most attractive features, what the poet Derek Mahon in his poem 'In Belfast' called 'the hill at the top of every street'.

No Place Like Home

The lamp-lighter was an evening visitor to most localities in Belfast until the early 1960s. Here he is in 1945 lighting a lamp in the Duncairn Gardens area of the city – even though the sun is shining! He usually travelled on a bicycle which, for the purpose of this photograph, appears to have been discreetly hidden. The Gilbey's sign behind him, where the onlookers are gathered, betokened a bar or off-licence.

HRH Princess Margaret unveiling a plaque in the City Hall commemorating the 350th anniversary of Belfast's charter of 1613, signifying its role in the Plantation of Ulster. In 1603 an English soldier named Arthur Chichester was granted 'the Castle of Bealfaste or Belfast', and the charter provided the Chichester family with the means to govern the town for the next two centuries. Prior to that, Belfast's main significance was strategic: it controlled a ford where the river could be crossed. In Irish, 'Beal Feirste' means 'the approach to the sandbank' which led to the crossing place.

The first 'Early Bird' satellite link-up shown in the Ulster Television 'Parade' programme in the 1970s between Belfast and the city of the same name in Maine, USA. As was the case with many towns in colonial America, arriving immigrants from Ireland, particularly Ulster, brought with them ready-made names for the settlements they established on arrival.

Like Edinburgh, Belfast is regarded by travel writers as one of the most picturesquely situated cities in the whole of Britain and Ireland. This photograph shows MacArt's Fort on top of Cave Hill, on the north shores of Belfast Lough, with fine views of the residential developments on the northern (County Antrim) and southern (County Down) sides, with the smoke in the middle rising from the city's industrial sites.

19

The Lagan Navigation, begun in the mid-eighteenth century, joined Belfast to Lough Neagh and greatly facilitated the town's consequent expansion as a regional centre of trade by easing the transportation of bulky goods to and from the prosperous Lagan Valley. Its significance, particularly for the carriage of coal, continued into the twentieth century, as demonstrated by this uncommon image of one of the many families who gained a living on and from it.

Andersonstown in the early years of the twentieth century. This pleasant rural image is a reminder that what today are integral parts of suburban Belfast – Andersonstown, Newtownbreda, Shaw's Bridge, Knock, Strandtown, Greenisland, Ligoneil, Whitehouse, Whitewell, Carnmoney – were less than one hundred years ago villages that would not have looked out of place anywhere in the Irish countryside.

Mitchell's Row, off Brown Square, 1912. At this time it was listed in the directories simply as 'four small houses', with no name or occupation listed for the occupants. It was one of the streets scheduled for refurbishment under the 1910 Improvement Scheme which was more or less forced on the Corporation by the recognition that private enterprise could not be relied on to build houses for the poor.

Sir Robert McConnell was responsible for the most ambitious housing schemes undertaken in the development of middle-class suburbs from the early years of the twentieth century. The detached houses he built at St James's Park, Ravenhill Park and Ormiston Park (shown here) provided suitably respectable residences for Belfast's upwardly mobile middle classes.

The bricks at the brickworks in Springfield Road retained their heat overnight, affording homeless men at least some warmth as they slept rough. This photograph was taken at 3.30 in the morning in the early years of the century, and was one of a series of images commissioned by the Belfast Central Mission to illustrate the extent of the problem of homelessness.

Belfast Corporation's record of public house building between the wars has often been criticised and was certainly the worst in Britain: only 2,600 houses were constructed. The last large-scale housing scheme for artisans in these years was at Glenard Park in Ardoyne, in the north-west of the city, completed in 1934–5. These houses (shown here) were certainly built to a better standard than had been evident earlier in the century. Each had a kitchen, a larder and, in the outside yard, a toilet and coal-shed. But only a narrow passage separated the houses at the back, no bathrooms were provided and the living space was little improved.

Virtually all the houses in Bombay Street were burned down on the night of 15 August 1969, the date most commonly associated with the onset of the Troubles. The Scarman Tribunal which reported on the events of August 1969 noted that 1,820 families had been forced to flee their homes, over 1,500 of them Catholic.

High-rise flats have long been dismissed as a solution to the mounting pressure for housing. The inadequacy of what were known as 'Weetabix' blocks was particularly evident on the Shankill Road and in the Divis Flats complex. Nevertheless this fourteen-storey development at Dunmurry on the outskirts of south-west Belfast, pictured here in 1975, indicates that in the right environment high-rise flats could work.

Riley's Court in the shadow of the gasworks in the Lower Ormeau Road area of the city, pictured on 19 May 1975. A common feature of inner-city housing in the last thirty years may be seen: the blocked up house, cheek by jowl with well-maintained houses scheduled for redevelopment. Such properties were principally inhabited by older people, most of whom had lived in one house all their lives.

The last surviving house in Conlig Street off the Shankill Road, *c.* 1980, stands as a defiant witness to the extensive shifts of population that characterised much of inner-city Belfast in the last quarter of the twentieth century.

Prefabricated 'Tin Towns', like this one on Belfast's Shore Road, built to counter postwar housing shortages, were a common feature of Blitz-torn cities across Britain. Originally intended as a short-term stop-gap, many were still being lived in until well into the 1960s. Here mothers protest at the appalling conditions they were forced to endure until the area was cleared in 1968 to make way for the M2 motorway linking Belfast with the north.

The sale of *The Big Issue* in all weathers by hardy vendors became an integral part of street activity in the 1990s. The Simon Community, set up in the city in 1971, has provided places of refuge for the increasing numbers, particularly of young people, who find themselves homeless.

Landmark & Locality

A Christmas card featuring the Town Clerk Robert Meyer, superimposed on the new City Hall, *c.* 1908, a period that might justifiably be seen as the apotheosis of Belfast's achievement. As historian Jonathan Bardon has said, 'it had the greatest shipyard, ropeworks, tobacco factory, linen spinning mill, dry dock and tea machinery works in the world'. It was about to embark on the building of the world's biggest ship, the *Titanic.* The opening of the City Hall in 1906 symbolised all this, and also marked Belfast's recent (1888) elevation to 'city' status.

Donegall Square North. The statues in the City Hall grounds include (nearest) the Royal Irish Rifles South African war memorial and (raised) a marble statue of Queen Victoria.

Clifton Street, looking towards Carlisle Circus, which is neatly framed by the imposing Gothic piles of St Enoch's Presbyterian Church, completed in 1872, and Carlisle Memorial Church. The latter was in fact the magnificent gift of one man, James Carlisle, in memory of his son.

Sandy Row has been traditionally regarded as the heartland of Protestant Belfast. This view also shows something of its other main characteristic: a busy shopping area 'where everybody knows your name'.

Dunville Park on the Falls Road, with the Royal Victoria Hospital in the background. The 4-acre site on the Falls Road was presented to the city in 1869 by Robert Dunville, whose family operated the city's main distilling concern. The remarkably fine terracotta Doulton Fountain in the foreground was erected by Robert Dunville in 1891 in memory of his sister Sara.

St Anne's Cathedral, 1932. The artist Miss Gertrude Martin is pictured with her designs for the mosaic of St Patrick in the cathedral, commissioned to mark the 1,500th anniversary of the traditionally accepted date of the arrival in Ireland of its patron saint.

The laying of the foundation stone of the Belfast Museum and Art Gallery on its Stranmillis Road site on 2 July 1924 by HRH the Duke of York.

The Botanic Garden was established on a 4-acre site in 1820 by the Royal Belfast Botanic and Horticultural Society. Its famous glass Palm House, finished in 1852, is now one of the oldest surviving examples of a curvilinear iron and glass structure anywhere.

Tate's Chemists, situated close to the main transport centre of Castle Junction, had been a familiar landmark on Royal Avenue since its development as Belfast's principal shopping thoroughfare in the 1880s.

The busy-ness of Lower North Street in 1926 suggests that bargains are to be found here. The queue on the left-hand side is outside the 'Two Ten Tailors' (whose suits cost, presumably, £2 10s), just beyond the White House which exhorts passers-by to 'Try Our Famous Ices'.

The Queens' Bridge, looking into east Belfast. On the right is the kiln of Ballymacarret Glassworks and on the left are tell-tale signs of the industry associated with the docks. The bridge had been widened in the 1880s as part of the thorough modernisation demanded by Belfast's position as the fastest growing city in the British Isles.

Photographed in 1935, the Blackstaff River and the gasworks cheek by jowl on the Ormeau Road, one of the main south-bound routes out of town.

33

The Alhambra Picture House, North Street, December 1937. It had been established in 1872 as the Alhambra Theatre by Dan Lowry, who had already opened similar variety halls in Liverpool and Manchester. At the time the photograph was taken, it had just opened, after conversion, as a picture house. It was appropriate that one of the first films it showed, *The Charge of the Light Brigade*, starred Errol Flynn, whose father had worked in Belfast before the war.

The Belfast Arts Theatre Company provided a useful forum for Ulster's playwrights and acting companies. Founded by Hubert and Dorothy Wilmot, who had come to Belfast in the 1930s, the Arts Theatre premises (seen here) opened in Botanic Avenue on 17 April 1961 with *Orpheus Descending* by Tennessee Williams. However, plays by local playwrights proved equally popular, particularly Sam Cree's *Second Honeymoon* and (advertised here) *Married Bliss*, farcical and self-deprecating commentaries on Ulster life. 'Let others write the "significant" plays so long as I can continue to keep people happy,' Cree is reported to have said.

The Odyssey, Northern Ireland's landmark Millennium Project which was taking shape at the very end of the twentieth century, not only embodied Belfast's commercial revival but also represented the attractions it had to offer, both for its own citizens and for the increasing number of visitors. The 'W5' – Who, What, When, Where, Why – provides a state-of-the-art science learning experience with whose early development the Ulster Museum was associated.

The zoological gardens at Bellevue in the 1930s provided an absorbing and accessible place to visit, easily reached by bus along the Antrim Road. It was seriously affected during the war when, after the major April air raid on the city, the Minister of Public Security John MacDermott took the decision, in response to public unease, to destroy the most dangerous animals. The *Belfast Newsletter* reported that, as thirty-two animals including lions, tigers, bears, wolves, vultures and a giant rat were shot, the head-keeper stood watching 'with tears streaming down his face, as the executioners proceeded from cage to cage'.

The Europa Hotel's stoical claim to fame throughout the 1970s and 1980s was that of being 'the most bombed hotel in Europe' (including Beirut). It also served as the main hostelry for the world's press who arrived to cover the stories emerging from the dark days of the Troubles, a clientele which surely could only have enhanced its attraction as a target for political terrorism.

The short-lived concrete fountain in Corn Market, one of the city's social hearts and oldest traditional meeting and gathering places, photographed on a sunny July afternoon in 1978. The road stretching directly behind leads to Castle Place, where the original 'Castle of Bealfast' purportedly stood.

The Albert Clock under wraps for refurbishment in 2000. Among the best known of the city's landmarks, the Albert Clock was designed by the local architect, W.J. Barre. The 113ft-high clock tower was built in 1865–9, and was called officially the Albert Memorial, in memory of Queen Victoria's late husband. Constructed on reclaimed land, it was soon noticed to be 'considerably out of plumb'. By 1900 it had acquired its characteristic Tower of Pisa tilt which, hopefully, the renovations will do little to rectify.

'Inst', the Royal Belfast Academical Institution, is regarded as being right at the heart of the city centre. The black and gold colours of the boys' uniforms (like many of the long-established schools in Northern Ireland – it was founded in 1810 – it remains single-sex) are a familiar sight, especially at the end of the school day when they generally move much faster than these two lads.

This stunning view of Belfast was taken from the roof of the Telephone Exchange soon after it opened in 1935. It shows the view westwards to May Street and the City Hall, with the mountains of Co. Antrim in the background. The slow shutter speed chosen by the photographer has allowed the lights of streetlamps and car headlights to blend into a glowing mass, giving this image its ethereal quality.

Royal Avenue, one of Belfast's main shopping streets and central thoroughfares, resplendently lit for Christmas 1990, with the bright lights of the new Virgin megastore drawing consumers to a range of music products previously undreamt of by local fans.

The new Lagan Weir, part of the massive waterfront redevelopment of Belfast's Laganside, pictured in the 1990s. John Kindness's fabulous mosaic statue of a salmon symbolises the regeneration both of the city and of the river on which it stands, newly repopulated with living examples of this kingly fish.

Buying & Selling

The interior of the shop at the Windsor Dairy on Belfast's Lisburn Road, *c.* 1910, with a hand-churn for making butter strategically placed in the foreground. The impact of tuberculosis was keenly felt when this photograph was taken as part of a city-wide campaign promoting hygienic practices in the preparation and distribution of animal produce, particularly milk and meat.

On a wet day there seems to be no reprieve for these turkeys obligingly allowing themselves to be carted off towards the market and a fate equivalent to a Christmas dinner.

A Belfast Co-operative Society horse-drawn bread van, well enough turned out to win second prize for its driver, Mr J. Blair.

The Belfast abattoir in Macauley Street, 1901. The manager was Mr W. Hoey, and presumably he's the man standing on the right, wearing the bowler hat. The public abattoir and the private slaughter-houses throughout the city were taken under the control of the City Council's Market Committee from the early years of the twentieth century. This was Belfast's first slaughterhouse, built in 1869. By the beginning of the twentieth century it had become inadequate but it was not until councillors had toured Europe as part of a long-running debate at Town Council level that a new slaughterhouse was built in 1913.

Department of Agriculture inspectors examining potatoes bound for export at Belfast docks, 11 January 1938. Though its industrial output was badly affected in the interwar period, much attention was given to improving the quality of local agricultural produce and its marketing. The notice on the wall invites farmers and Young Farmers' Clubs to participate in a 'New Variety Potato Growing Competition' in 1938. Less wholesomely, the smaller one-line notice states 'No Spitting'.

A piano, however rickety, for 3½d was an extraordinary bargain even by the standards of Smithfield Market. No doubt the catch became clear when you followed the invitation to 'see inside'. The 1960s gents' hairstyles suggest that a 'spiv' is close at hand.

Modern street traders selling a range of novelty socks on a stall in Castle Place. Although some bad feeling has been aroused by these unlicensed traders, many feel that the colour and entertainment they add to a rapidly homogenising city shopping environment is well worth a bit of litter and noise.

The staff of Anderson & McAuley's department store, one of Belfast's most illustrious shopping venues, arranged in Cecil B. de Mille fashion on its famous staircase.

Samples of what appear to be under-garments liberally bedeck the hosiery department of Anderson & McAuley's in pre-war days. From its prestigious position commanding the busy Castle Junction, it specialised in the sale of goods made from locally produced linen, to the extent that it could claim that 'purchasers have to pay no intermediate profits between the manufacturer and the retailer'.

W. Erskine Mayne's bookshop at
the corner of Chichester Street and
Donegall Square East was for many
years one of the city's shopping
landmarks. It was begun in 1815 as
an initiative of evangelical clergymen
and by 1833 had removed to this site,
where it was managed by Mr Alex
S. Mayne, agent for, among others,
the British and Foreign Bible Society
and the Hibernian Bible Society. This
mid-1930s window display features
recent books on nature, history, poetry
and theology as well as the 'epic of
indomitable courage' on the 1933
expedition to Everest.

The 'Tele' sellers with their distinctive and, to the uninitiated, virtually incomprehensible
cries have been part of the street life of Belfast's city centre for generations of passers-by.

A welcome cup of tea for busy stall-holders in Belfast's St George's Market in 1990. The last of a wide variety of city commodity markets to survive, its weekly displays of clothing, fruit and vegetables, bric-a-brac and other goods continue to attract shoppers and retailers from far and near.

The interior of one of Belfast's most-loved buildings, the Insurance building 'with the heads' on Donegall Square South, photographed in its most recent reincarnation as an up-market delicatessen and café.

McKenna's Bar on Stanfield Street, photographed on 19 May 1975, when these street-corner 'local' city pubs were already becoming rare. The large metal doors behind the parked car belong to the Stewart Street depot of Belfast Corporation Transport Department, where several of the 'drivers' listed as living in Stanfield Street were doubtless employed.

Forster Green's Tea Shop, at the corner of Royal Avenue and North Street, was listed in the trade directory as 'wholesale and retail grocers and Italian warehousemen'. This Quaker family endowed the Forster Green Hospital for Consumption and Chest Diseases in a 45-acre site in Knockbreda in south Belfast. In 1907 the Belfast Corporation undertook to maintain thirty-five beds in the hospital, in acknowledgement of the serious extent of respiratory diseases in its population.

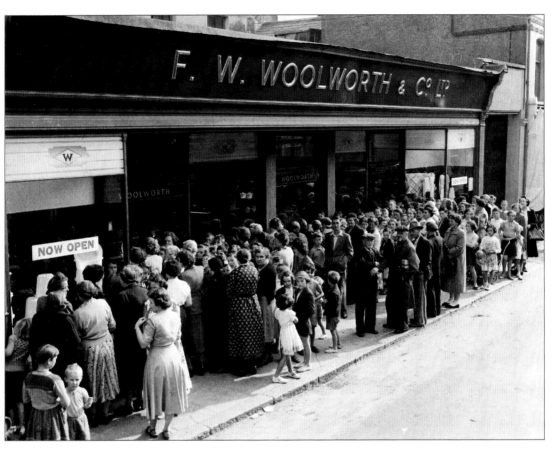

Even though it says it is 'Now Open', this Woolworth's store in North Street is still keeping its expectant queues of shoppers waiting in the sunshine on a late July day in 1955. This store was first built in the 1920s, so it might be reopening after renovations rather than for the summer sales. Would the 'Broken Biscuit' counter have been repaired?

Belfast's Castle Court retail complex, shown here decorated for its first Christmas in 1990, was built on land freed by the demolition of the city's famous Grand Central Hotel. The opening of the new complex caused hearts to leap among dedicated shoppers, who could now be tempted by such national high-street giants as Debenhams and Gap, and it marked a new rebirth in city centre fortunes.

Making & Doing

A carter homeward plods his weary way at Forthriver brickworks, *c.* 1930.

WORLD'S RIVETING RECORD
WORKMAN CLARK—JUNE 1918

	NUMBER OF RIVETS	ACCUMULATING TOTALS
1ST HOUR	1167	1167
2ND ..	1101	2268
3RD ..	1071	3339
4TH ..	1187	4526
5TH ..	1267	5793
6TH ..	1328	7121
7TH ..	1409	8530
8TH ..	1276	9806
9TH ..	1403	11209
TOTAL		

This is a photograph of the board on which was recorded the hour by hour totals of rivets driven home by J. Moir, and include only the actual numbers as passed by Lloyds and British Corporation Surveyors.

Workman Clark are very proud of the skill and organisation which resulted in the tremendous total of 11,209 rivets by one man in a working day, a Shipbuilding record which will probably stand for all time.

Testimony to the record-breaking number of rivets driven in by one worker, J. Moir, in one day in 1918 in the Workman Clark shipyard. The two Belfast shipyards of Workman Clark and Harland & Wolff led the response of British shipyards in the last two years of the First World War to the challenge that arose from shipping losses at the hands of Germany's U-boats. The herculean efforts of Workman Clark's riveters at this time were legendary. Riveters were, with caulkers and platers, among the aristocracy of shipyard workers, in 1916 earning 2*s* 6*d* per day. Note the nine-hour working day.

A fine body of men, the Harland & Wolff East Yard riveters. The achievements of the two yards in the First and of Harland & Wolff in the Second World War (Workman Clark had gone into liquidation in 1935) have been generally masked by the self-deprecating humour which was a characteristic of the sub-culture of the shipyards. The usual droll response to the question 'How many people work in Harland & Wolff?' was 'About half of them'!

This remarkable photograph was taken from the foc'sle of the Union Castle liner *Capetown Castle* as the ship prepared for launch on 23 September 1937 and well demonstrates the sheer scale of activity at the Harland & Wolff shipyard which built her. Far below, workers swarm like tiny ants to see off their latest achievement.

McAnally's blacksmith's forge at Ballyhackamore in east Belfast. The proprietor, McAnally himself, is on the left. The boy, named Vance, with his back to the camera, was 12½ years old. As well as shoeing horses, McAnally specialised in making railings, including those around the City Hall, which were melted down and reused during the Second World War.

A tea-drying turbine made by Sirocco Engineering Works. The idea for this enterprise arose from Samuel Davidson's training on his uncle's tea plantations in northern India. Taking the name from the Sirocco wind, in the 1880s Davidson patented the design for drying tea, inaugurated the engineering manufactory at Ballymacarret and developed means of transporting the equipment to India, where he himself retained connections with the tea-growing industry. At the beginning of the century the Sirocco Works had become the world leader in ventilation and fan manufacture.

Fishing lines being made at Belfast Ropeworks, 1899. Overhead is a 'Belfast roof,' a distinctive local construction using timber trellis.

Jacquard weaving in Donegall Road linen mill, *c.* 1920.

The Hughes-Dickson Flour Mill on the Falls Road. Bernard Hughes had arrived in Belfast from Co. Armagh by the early 1830s and quickly became established as a major entrepreneur in the provision of bread for the city's population, particularly when the potato crop failed so calamitously in the late 1840s. His innovative ideas provided cheaper bread for Belfast's growing population, immortalised in the famous 'Barney's Baps' which formed a staple diet for much of the city's workforce. Hughes's other claim to fame is that he was the first Catholic representative elected to Belfast Corporation.

Icing cakes at the Ormeau Bakery. The first of a number of local bakeries to provide 'fancy bread' and cakes for the collective sweet tooth of the Belfast population, the Ormeau Bakery was begun in 1875 by Robert Wilson, and was located initially at 90–92 Cromac Street. When it moved to new and extended premises in 1890, it took its name from its location at the junction of Ormeau Road and Ava Street.

The staff of Caffrey's brewery, pictured on the opening of new premises at Andersonstown, south-west Belfast (now the Glen Road), in 1905. The business had relocated there from Smithfield in central Belfast.

A craftsman roughly shaping the clay in Hamilton's Clay Pipe Factory in Waterford Street, off the Falls Road, *c.* 1914.

Hand-stripping the tobacco leaf at Gallaher's Tobacco Manufacturers, York Street, in the 1950s. The five-storey factory at York Street had been erected in 1881 and at the turn of the century employed over 600 hands. Thomas Gallaher retained a very hands-on management approach: the directory entry said that he 'personally supervises every detail of the trade' and that his 'prestige as a tobacco grower and manufacturer is widely and freely acknowledged'.

The compositors' room at the *Belfast Telegraph* Royal Avenue offices. Begun in 1870 by W. and G. Baird, it commanded a province-wide readership, its delivery vans a familiar and fearsome sight on the roads, screeching to a halt at newsagents and departing just as quickly.

Designers at McCaw Stevenson & Orr at work in their Linenhall Street offices, draughting artwork for the posters, labels, illuminated addresses and letter-headed paper, all of which would become something of an art form in themselves.

Before starring in the BBC Z *Cars* series in the 1960s and the 'Billy' trilogy of plays by Graham Reid in the 1980s, Belfast-born James Ellis had been involved in the city's famous Group Theatre and, as shown here, in the Ulster Television series *Heads or Harps*.

William Conor was the son of a tinsmith and gasfitter, but by the time he died in Salisbury Avenue aged 87 in 1968, he was probably the most popular and representative Belfast painter of his generation. MAGNI is privileged to have in its care a wide range of his paintings and drawings in both the Ulster Folk & Transport Museum and the Ulster Museum.

Two of the city's foremost literary alumni. The poet John Hewitt, formerly Keeper of Art in the Ulster Museum, reading a volume of poetry by Seamus Heaney, a member of the Department of English at the Queen's University from the late 1960s until the mid-1970s and winner of the 1995 Nobel Prize for Literature.

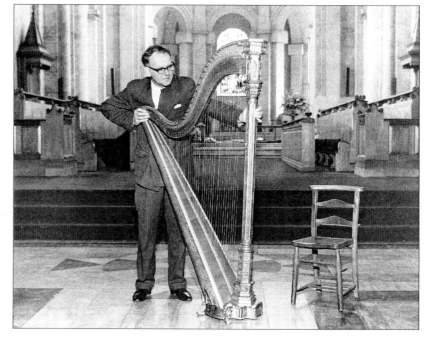

As teacher, broadcaster, musician and conductor, Havelock Nelson was the 'Mr Music' of Belfast. His influence lives on in the provision of an excellent School of Music and in the worldwide recognition given to the Ulster Orchestra.

James Young, who died in 1974, is fondly remembered for his stage appearances and radio and TV broadcasts, in which he poked fun at the people of Belfast, particularly their accents and least-becoming social characteristics, and for his constant exhortation to 'stop fightin'!

Frank McFadden, pictured at his home and workshop, 22 Dunstan Street, Springfield Avenue, 1 August 1973. An expert player of the *uilleann* pipes, he also specialised in their manufacture and maintenance, exemplified in the Egan set held in the Ulster Museum, which he restored.

Part of a growing band of street entertainers, this accordionist proudly fills his regular Castle Place venue with airs to please and tease.

Coming & Going

Would you say this man was a porter, carrying luggage off an incoming boat at Belfast docks, or is he perhaps a returned emigrant, coming home from a job in England?

Castle Junction, where Royal Avenue meets Castle Place, remained the focal point of the city's transport system throughout the twentieth century. Here old and new forms of transport – electrified trams and horse-drawn vehicles – appear to be living in harmony on a sunny day, while inhabitants perambulate in the sunshine, the ladies in their finery.

Opposite, below: Workmen in Donegall Square laying the tramlines to be used in the electrification of the city's tramway system, *c.* 1905. The hoardings in the background announce the current attractions at two of the city's most famous theatres, the Empire and the Theatre Royal.

The construction and maintenance of the trams that served Belfast, crucial to ensuring the effective working of the transport system which served a population of 350,000 in the early years of the century, called for a well-equipped workshop, including forges.

Everyone is taking very seriously the instructions to 'Keep Left' at this new roundabout at Arthur Square in the early 1930s. Even the men in charge of the handcarts and the cyclist have taken their place in what threatens to become a never-ending circuitous procession intent on . . . keeping left.

The new Sydenham by-pass, designed to improve traffic into and out of Belfast from Holywood, Bangor and the North Down dormitory belt, being tested – but by pedestrians and a dog rather than by motorists.

The Foster family at Belfast Harbour before emigrating in April 1929, probably to Australia or Canada.

The Vallely family before taking ship as emigrants, also in 1929. These photographs were part of a series taken by McCalla Travel Agents in Belfast. Looking at these poignant images of families setting out for a New World, it is difficult not to wonder how things turned out for them, particularly the children.

Another 'biggest in the world' claim for Belfast. The Belfast Rope Work Company at Connswater, from which these workers are emerging at the end of a long day in about 1905, had a workforce well in excess of 1,500 people by the 1890s, and was recognised as being the largest such company in the world. It continued to expand and just before the outbreak of war in 1914 it employed an estimated 3,000.

A rush of shipyard workers intent on leaving Queen's Island along Hamilton Road at the end of a working day in 1954, using whatever transport is available – on foot, bike, motorbike, car or bus. The ships *Raeburn* and *Pontia* in the background are in the Musgrave Channel, later the site of the building dock.

An air crash at Balmoral, then on the outskirts of the city! The back of this postcard bears the inscription 'Showing the ill-fated machine with Mr Valentine and Mr Dunville to right of card, 21 September 1912'.

The very first stages in the establishment of what was to become Belfast International Airport at Aldergrove in south Co. Antrim were fired by the need for Harland & Wolff's to build runways of sufficient length to test the aircraft they were building for the First World War effort. This photograph was taken in early 1918 when the steel hangars were under construction. One wonders to whom (or to what?) the warning sign was addressed.

Rex McCandless, the famous Belfast inventor of the 'featherbed' frame for the Norton Motorcycle company, seen here in his autogyro. The problems of stability that bedevilled these flying machines meant that the craft never went into commercial production. However, several models were made, from the prototype with its Triumph Twin motorcycle engine to the production version powered by a Volkswagen car engine.

The launch of the *Capetown Castle* in September 1937. The ship eventually left Queen's Island in March 1938 for service with the Union Castle line, who commissioned a long series of 'Castle' ships from Harland & Wolff over the years. The *Capetown Castle* was requisitioned by the Admiralty in 1942 for conversion to an aircraft carrier. Fittingly, she returned to Harland & Wolff's in 1946 for reconversion once her active war service was over.

Some Events & Occasions

These dancers, in full swing on the Bangor boat, are workers celebrating the opening in 1906 of the new United Cooperative Bakery on Ravenhill Road.

In September 1902 a
combination of torrential
rain, heavy autumnal tides
and the inadequacy of the
city's drainage and sewage
schemes resulted in large
parts of Belfast flooding to
a depth of several feet. The
deluge caused widespread
disruption for traffic and
commuters, but here some
Belfast youngsters have
been caught by the camera
finding, as children will,
their own amusement in the
troubles of adults.

Firemen could be forgiven
for suspecting a hoax
after being called out to
extinguish a fire in this
fireplace shop in Boyne
Street on Belfast's Sandy
Row in 1968.

Children celebrating May Day and fêting their May Queen on Belfast's Cave Hill Road in 1916.

Members of Ballynafeigh Fire Brigade dressed for fundraising, c. 1900.

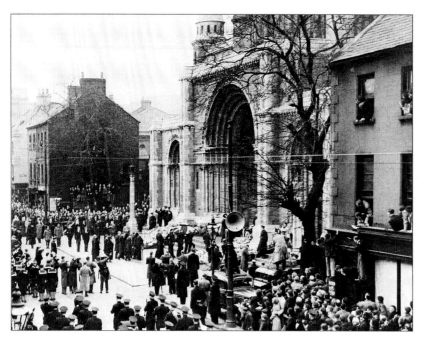

The state funeral of Lord Carson at St Anne's Cathedral, 26 October 1935. Born in Dublin, Sir Edward Carson came to prominence for the oratorical skills he displayed at the trial of Oscar Wilde, an ability he also used in orchestrating the Unionist opposition to Home Rule. He remains the only person to have been buried in St Anne's. He is also believed to be the only British politician to have been present at the unveiling of his own statue, a ceremony that took place at Stormont in 1933.

The funeral of Lord Craigavon in 1940. In June 1921 Sir James Craig had become the first Prime Minister of Northern Ireland, having taken over the leadership of the Ulster Unionists from Sir Edward Carson in February that year. Born in Belfast, he served as a captain in the Royal Irish Rifles in the Boer War before entering politics in 1906 as MP for East Down. He became something of a part-time Prime Minister, whose cruises to other parts of the British Empire were justified on grounds of ill-health.

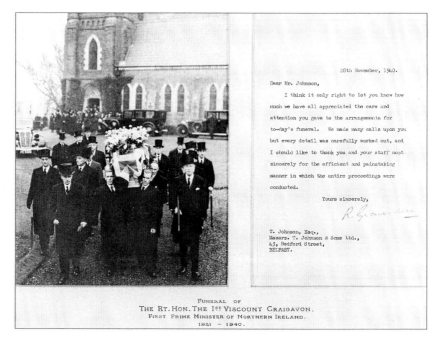

28th November, 1940.

Dear Mr. Johnson,

    I think it only right to let you know how much we have all appreciated the care and attention you gave to the arrangements for to-day's funeral. We made many calls upon you but every detail was carefully worked out, and I should like to thank you and your staff most sincerely for the efficient and painstaking manner in which the entire proceedings were conducted.

Yours sincerely,

R. Gransden

T. Johnson, Esq.,
Messrs. T. Johnson & Sons Ltd.,
43, Bedford Street,
BELFAST.

FUNERAL OF
THE RT. HON. THE 1ST VISCOUNT CRAIGAVON.
FIRST PRIME MINISTER OF NORTHERN IRELAND.
1921 — 1940.

Goanese seamen parade through Belfast's docklands in April 1959 to honour their patron saint, Francis of Assisi.

A special occasion indeed, with sustenance for body as well as spirit given the spread provided, was the unveiling of the new Campbell Street Mission Sunday School banner in the Alderdice Hall in 1926. Fired with evangelical zeal, the charitable activities of local missions such as this made a real difference to the lives of many poor Belfast children.

Commemoration at McArt's Fort in 1963 of the 165th anniversary of the 1798 Rebellion. It was here in May 1795 that the United Irishmen had met and, in the words of Wolfe Tone, one of their leaders, 'took a solemn obligation never to desist in our efforts until we had subverted the authority of England over our country and asserted her independence'. After the rebellion had failed, the local hero Henry Joy McCracken took refuge here on the slopes of Cave Hill, sustained by food brought to him by his sister Mary Ann. He was caught and hanged in Corn Market on 17 July 1798.

Opposite, top: My Lady's Road colourfully decorated for the visit to Belfast of George VI in 1937 following his coronation.
Opposite, below: The residents of North Thomas Street on 12 July 1959 as they wait for the parades to pass.

Under the supervision of Miss Sadie Prentice and overlooked by his wife, Lord Brookeborough, Prime Minister of Northern Ireland, tries his hand at making a trawl net at the Belfast Ropeworks' display at the Festival of Britain Exhibition in Montgomery Road during the summer of 1951.

During her visit to Northern Ireland in 1950 Princess Elizabeth found time to inspect prize-winning cattle at the Royal Ulster Agricultural Society's show at Balmoral, accompanied by the Revd and Rt Hon. R. Moore, Minister for Agriculture in the Northern Irish government.

A rare sight indeed as elephants from Chipperfields Circus parade down Garmoyle Street in Belfast's Sailortown. It is difficult to imagine such a spectacle happening today – perhaps the streets were more exciting in the past.

The launch of the American-designed drilling rig *Sea Quest* was a triumph of technical achievement for Harland & Wolff's. This was the first time any oil rig – let alone the largest so far constructed – had been launched complete, and it called for three separate slipways to be built, one for each leg. It seemed that the whole of Belfast came out to hold their breath and then cheer with relief as the mighty structure first wobbled and then safely entered the water on 7 January 1966.

Ordered in 1957, the *Canberra* was the biggest passenger liner built in a British shipyard since the *Princess Elizabeth*, and represented the most valuable contract ever awarded to Harland & Wolff. So soundly designed and constructed was this outstanding vessel, pictured here at her launch on 14 April 1960, that she stayed in service for thirty-six years; even today, her riveted frames and seams defy attempts to break her for scrap.

The launch of any ship was a cause for celebration and a few hours' break for the workers of Queen's Island. Here, some of the men who helped put together the *Canberra* wait to see her down the slipway and out to sea.

Edward VII and Queen Alexandra arriving at the entrance to the grounds of the City Hall in 1903 to unveil the statue of Queen Victoria which stood in pride of place at the front of the richly decorated new building.

Members of the Northern Ireland football team leaving Belfast en route for Sweden, where they reached the quarter-finals of the 1958 World Cup finals. Standing at the front is Bertie Peacock, two behind him is Billy Bingham, and behind him is Danny Blanchflower, captain of the team. All three later managed the Northern Ireland team at various times. Under the astute management of Bingham, Northern Ireland again reached the World Cup finals, in 1982 (Spain) and 1986 (Mexico).

George Best acknowledging the acclaim of the crowd at Windsor Park in December 1986, at a testimonial match for the great Northern Ireland goalkeeper Pat Jennings, who had played over a hundred times for his country. Best, widely regarded as one of the most accomplished footballers of all time, had gone straight from Belfast to Manchester United as a young boy and had played in their European Cup-winning team in 1968. He won thirty-seven caps for Northern Ireland.

From 1961 to 1969 Sheila Murnaghan, a Dublin-born barrister and politician, served as the Liberal member of the Northern Ireland parliament for Queen's University, the only Liberal ever to do so. A member of the first Northern Ireland Community Relations Commission, she was also the driving force behind the campaign to have Northern Ireland's first Human Rights Bill enacted.

Wars & Rumours of Wars

Although labelled by the photographer, W.A. Green, as the 'Irish Rifles Statue', this statue at Belfast City Hall in fact commemorates the troops from Belfast and counties Antrim and Down who served in the Royal Irish Rifles during the Boer War Campaign in South Africa from 1899 to 1902. Modelled by Sydney March of London, it was unveiled by General Lord Grenfell on 6 October 1906. It carries plaques listing 1,219 members of the Royal Irish Rifles and 13 of the London Irish Rifles, who died in South Africa.

War charity match. Two sides, somewhat awkwardly labelled the 'English War Team' and the 'Irish War Team', competed in a charity match at Windsor Park, Belfast, towards the end of the First World War in aid of the Prisoners of War Fund and the Ulster Volunteer Force Hospital.

Soldiers of the 14th Battalion of the Royal Irish Rifles, formerly the Young Citizens' Volunteers, take a break during training on the outskirts of Belfast before embarking for France in the early days of the First World War. The part played by the 36th (Ulster) Division on 1 and 2 July, the opening days of the Battle of the Somme, has become legendary. Four VCs were won and some five thousand men were killed or wounded.

WAR CH

In aid of Prisoners of War

ENGLISH WAR TEAM
AT WINDSOR PARK 12TH

(Back Row) J.McPherson, Sergt Bell, J.English, Corpl Fenwick, J.Laurence, J.Rutherford, J.Cook, Corpl Tidswell, W.H.Allen
(TRAINER) (SUNDERLAND) (SHEFFIELD U) (WEST HAM) (NEWCASTLE U) (ARSENAL) (MIDDLESBORO) (REFEREE)
(Front Row) Lieut Gregory, W.Hibbert, F.Chambers, G.Hunter, Marquis of Londonderry, W.McCracken, H.Featherstone, G.Holley, D.Brooks
(NEWCASTLE U) (LIVERPOOL) (ASTON VILLA) (NEWCASTLE U) (ST MIRREN) (SUNDERLAND)

Y   MATCH
and U.V.F Hospital.

IRISH   WAR   TEAM
RESULT   SCORELESS   DRAW

ck Row)
C.Watson   J.MacBride.   J.Barron. A.McCluskey   H.D.Allen.
ddle Row)   SEC IFA   W.Lacey. H.Leddy   E.Scott   R.Mills   J.Scraggs   W.Gibson   R.Torrens.
nt Row) J.Wilgar.   D.Rollo. W.Emerson, Councl Gaffiken Marquis of Londonderry. J.Warwick.   E.Brooks D.Lyner.   M.Hamill.

A bustling and bedecked High Street in the late afternoon (the Albert Clock, that well-known local landmark at the foot of the street, says a quarter past four) on Peace Day, August 1919.

Public toilets in the city being sandbagged before the air raids of April and May 1941.

The engineering capacity of the Harland & Wolff shipyard was adapted during the Second World War for the manufacture not only of ships but also of aeroplanes and tanks, as seen here.

The manufacture of linen air cloth in Ewart's mill, 1943.

Don't ask how these aeroplanes got into Blitz Square, High Street, as part of 'Wings for Victory' week in Belfast in April 1943 . . . or how they got them out again! On the left is a Stirling bomber, on the right a Halifax.

Children fraternising with soldiers of the 34th US Infantry Division, the first contingent of American troops to arrive in Belfast (and also the first in Europe), 26 January 1942.

Something of the desolation caused by the second major German air raid on the city, on the night of 7 May 1941, is evident in this view of Bridge Street.

Digging among the rubble in the wake of an air raid. In the raid on the night of 15/16 April 1941, more were killed in one night – over 900 – than in any other city outside London.

A street party held in Ogilvie Street, off the Woodstock Road, in east Belfast to celebrate the end of the Second World War. Paper hats, flags, buns but only one man? . . . presumably the pubs were open.

General Dwight D. Eisenhower, here accompanied by the Lord Mayor, Sir Crawford McCullagh, visited Belfast on 24 August 1945 to receive the Freedom of the City. 'I have received honours in a number of cities,' he said, 'but never have I been more impressed with the sincerity and friendliness exhibited towards me than in Belfast.'

Led by local activist Andy Barr, the Campaign for Nuclear Disarmament marched through Custom House Square in protest against the arrival in Belfast of the ballistic missile submarine HMS *Renown* (seen opposite), shortly after her launch in March 1968.

The Butler family, waiting to be evacuated to the countryside. Remarkably, at the end of the century, nearly sixty years later, all the members of the family were still alive, save for the eldest girl, standing at the back holding the baby. Given the well-groomed appearance evident here, it comes as something of a surprise that provincial towns welcoming other evacuees from Belfast were shocked by their poverty and social habits. A civil servant administering the evacuation scheme wrote of 'such quantities of fleas, such lousy little Protestants, such nitty young RCs'.

Troubles & Strife

Political graffiti with a difference. A *cri de coeur* carefully painted on a wall at the junction of Bond Street with McAuley Street in the Markets district of the city. Oliver Plunkett, Roman Catholic Archbishop of Armagh, was executed in London on 1 July 1681 following accusations, later proved to be wholly false, that he had been involved in the 'Popish Plot' and had assisted in plans for a French invasion. For his martyrdom, he was made a saint by the Roman Catholic Church in 1975.

The opposition to Home Rule among the Unionist population in Ireland reached its height on Ulster Day, 28 September 1912. The crowds here are queuing at the City Hall to sign the Solemn League and Covenant. Signatories were admitted in batches of 500, with 150 signing every minute. In the event, the measure was set aside when the First World War broke out in August 1914.

The Unionist concerns at the introduction of Home Rule, which they equated with 'Rome Rule', went as far as establishing a provisional government for the predominantly Unionist counties in the north-east of Ireland which had consistently opposed the moves towards the introduction of Home Rule.

The Northern Ireland parliament was opened on 22 June 1921 by King George V. Here the royal procession is leaving Belfast City Hall. Rioting and civil strife made for a tense background to their majesties' presence. 'I can't tell you how glad I am I came,' the king confided in James Craig, the Prime Minister of the new Northern Ireland government, 'but you know my entourage were very much against it.'

A Jeffrey-Quad armoured
car on the streets of
Belfast in 1920, in
response to the street
clashes and civil unrest
that accompanied the
political uncertainty in
the immediate aftermath
of the ending of the First
World War, when these
cars first saw service.

In a scene more usually associated with Belfast in the 1970s and 1980s, British army soldiers and members of the Royal Ulster Constabulary carry out a street search of civilians at the junction of Royal Avenue and Kent Street in the spring of 1922. The RUC had just been established and, in keeping with the exceptional times, the new Special Powers Act gave it exceptional powers to detain suspects and set up courts of summary jurisdiction.

Opposite: Firemen struggling to contain the fire which had broken out at Levy's York Road premises on a Sunday evening in early July 1922. The political and sectarian upheavals which accompanied the Partition of Ireland in 1920–2 were most evident in Belfast. In 1921 over a hundred were killed; the intensity of the street battles in 1922 are evident in the statistics for May alone when 44 Catholics and 22 Protestants met with violent deaths. Only a few days prior to the arson attack on Levy's, the Irish Civil War had broken out with the shelling of the Four Courts in Dublin. Hereafter, IRA activity in Belfast was diverted.

These unemployed men are queuing in High Street on 15 March 1933 for the Assisted Dog Licensing Fund. The notice in the window reads 'Applicants for Assisted Dog Licences must apply in person and pay 2/6 at 57b High Street on Wednesday 15th March at 3pm. No claims will be considered after this date. Applicants who are in employment need not apply.' The large number of applicants reflects the fact that at this time over 30 per cent of the city's workforce was unemployed.

A dinner was held on 30 June 1932 in the Grand Central Hotel in support of Fascism in Italy. Later in the 1930s Belfast and County Down would provide a refuge for members of Jewish families fleeing Nazi Europe.

A demonstration at the Whitla Hall was arranged by Queen's University students on 14 October 1968 to coincide with Prime Minister O'Neill's visit to present prizes to pupils of the nearby Methodist College. The People's Democracy movement, consisting mainly of students and campaigning on a series of issues, including gerrymandering (hence the 'Fair Boundaries' poster), had been set up in Queen's University only a few days before.

The Prime Minister of Northern Ireland, Captain Terence O'Neill, taking part in a local television broadcast, entitled *Celtic Challenge*, with local students. O'Neill's invitation to the Taoiseach of the Republic of Ireland, Sean Lemass, to visit and hold talks in Belfast in January 1965 was one of a number of initiatives intended to foster better relations between north and south which attracted much public attention and debate before the Troubles erupted in the summer of 1969.

Opposite: The original Special Powers Act, the focus of this dignified though slightly sheepish public protest in West Belfast in the early 1970s, actually dates from 1922. It was augmented by a series of additional powers in the 1970s and 1980s in response to the continued paramilitary threat to public order.

Burnt-out houses in Farringdon Gardens, Ardoyne, in August 1971; the fleeing families are gathering up a few surviving effects to take with them. Intimidation and fear were rampant: 2 per cent of the 45,000 Catholic households in the city and 0.5 per cent of the 135,000 Protestant households were displaced in a matter of weeks in the summer and autumn of 1971, ensuring the collapse of long-held hopes of inter-communal housing.

Opposite, below: Graffiti in the Belfast Protestant community, representing the fear of previous generations that 'Home Rule is Rome Rule'.

A kaleidoscope of Republican sources of concern squeezed on to a fence at Colligan Street on the Springfield Road: the Revd Ian Paisley, the 'B' Specials, the Royal Ulster Constabulary and the attacks on Catholic quarters by Loyalists in August 1969 that are widely regarded as marking the onset of nearly thirty years of 'Troubles'.

A Republican march on the Falls Road in 1973, whose primary bone of contention was the powers of Special Courts. The context for their growing concern was that, two years earlier, over 600 people believed to have been associated with the Republican movement had been interned, not having been charged with any specific felony. This was one of a series of measures taken by the Stormont government which preceded its suspension in March 1972. The 'Whitelaw' referred to in the poster was Willie (later Lord) Whitelaw, the first Secretary of State for Northern Ireland, a position he had taken up when the government of Northern Ireland had been assumed by Westminster in what would become known as 'Direct Rule'.

Houses in New Bond Street in the Markets area being searched by the British army in January 1972 following the escape of Republican detainees from the prison ship in Belfast Lough, HMS *Maidstone*. This ship had held suspects arrested without charge when internment was introduced in August 1971.

The incoming Northern Ireland Executive, seen at Stormont on 31 December 1973, the day before taking office. Under Prime Minister Brian Faulkner (third from right) it represented the decisions reached in the Sunningdale Agreement in November 1973 to create a government which gave for the first time representation proportionally to the two major traditions, Unionists and Nationalist, in Northern Ireland. It lasted until it was brought down by the general strike led by the Ulster Workers' Council in May 1974.

Members of the Royal Ulster Constabulary in riot gear regaining control of the Shankill Road on 11 October 1969, but not before the rioters had left in their wake a trail of burning and burnt-out cars. The serious disturbances arose from street protests following the publication of the Hunt Report, which recommended the disbandment of the 'B' Specials and the disarming of the RUC. Constable Victor Arbuckle, a 29-year-old married officer with two children, was mortally wounded during the riots – the first policeman to be killed in the Troubles.

A riot in North Belfast in the 1970s, sparked off by opposition to the route taken by an Orange parade. In more recent times disputes over respective 'rights' – of Loyalists to march and of Catholic communities to have a say in the choice of the procession's route, particularly if it passes through their sector – have generally provoked street unrest only when negotiations at community level have broken down.

Soldiers about to scoop up in a most undignified manner the statue of the 'Roaring' Revd Hugh Hanna, which was blown up at Carlisle Circus in October 1969. Although it survived the fall largely intact, it has never been restored. An icon of nineteenth-century evangelical Protestantism in Belfast, Hanna was the founder of the nearby St Enoch's Presbyterian Church in Clifton Street. He died in 1892 and his memorial was erected two years later.

Malone House in Barnett's Park, south Belfast, was bombed on 11 November 1976. The Ulster Museum's fine collection of costume and textiles, stored there at the time, was destroyed. An early seventeenth-century embroidered jacket, some superb eighteenth-century costumes and the third most highly rated collection of linen damask in the world were among the many significant losses. A new collection has been created.

Smithfield, Belfast's most famous market, was destroyed by fire in May 1974. Even the indomitable Joseph 'I buy anything' Kavanagh was put out of action, however temporarily. Smithfield Market was never rebuilt.

Opposite, below: Jokes about the inconvenience caused by the closure during the Troubles of public . . . er, conveniences have long lost any impact they might once have had, even as toilet humour.

Security barriers at the corner of Berry Street and Chapel Lane, 1972. What became an accepted part of 'normal' life for the inhabitants from the early 1970s until the mid-1990s never ceased to fascinate, even appal, visitors to the city.

Mairead Corrigan with her brother-in-law Jackie Maguire, whose three children were killed at Finaghy in a terrorist-related incident in August 1976, sparking off the formation of the Peace People. Ms Corrigan, who was awarded the 1976 Nobel Prize for Peace, donated her medal to the Ulster Museum. When Mrs Maguire subsequently died, Mairead married Mr Maguire.

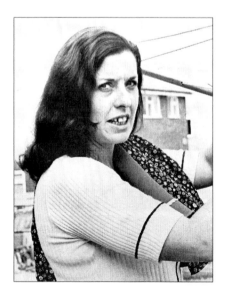

Betty Williams witnessed the horrific incident in which the three Maguire children were killed. Together with Mairead Corrigan, the children's aunt, and Ciaran McKeown she was instrumental in forming the Peace People, the first peace movement to articulate successfully, if briefly, the public concern at the mounting waste of human life. She too was awarded the Nobel Prize for Peace. She later moved to live in the United States. *Lost Lives*, which relates the stories of the men, women and children who died as a result of the Northern Ireland Troubles, describes the Peace People as being 'generally remembered in Belfast as a transient phenomenon with powerful initial impetus but which in the end did not deliver the peace it sought to bring about'.

Benny's Bar, at the corner of Garmoyle and Ship Street, in the Docks area, was the scene of a tragic explosion on the night of 31 October 1972. Four-year-old Clare Hughes and six-year-old Paula Stronge were killed by a bomb as they played around a Hallowe'en bonfire. Nine years later three men were convicted for the atrocity, and the judge told them: 'Two innocent little children playing their Hallowe'en games in the street were killed. This will haunt you for the rest of your lives.'

An action shot, as it were, of RUC officers running towards a house in Osborne Gardens, off the Malone Road, where gunmen were reported to be holding hostages, in late August 1976.

Opposite, below: Army checkpoints became perhaps the most tedious aspect of 'normal' life during the Troubles. Civilian exasperation was best summed up in a television advert in which a driver clambered out of his car on a wet night to open the boot for inspection, giving vent vociferously to his view that the soldiers would be better deployed if only they cleared off to 'catch a few terrorists'.

The soldier with the shades on patrol at Staunton Street on a fine spring day in 1975 seems prepared to ignore the attentions of female admirers so that the cameraman gets his best side.

As with all peace lines built since 1969, the Peace Line that has been built in North Belfast, here photographed in April 1993, has been as much a blot on the landscape as it has symbolised the gaps in mutual understanding and trust between loyalist and nationalist communities in what is the most divided area of the city.

Acknowledgements & Picture Credits

The authors welcome this opportunity to acknowledge the substantial debt they owe to people from whose help they benefited. The professionalism of Anne Bennett, Sarah Cook and Michelle Tilling of Sutton Publishing helped reduce a near-impossible deadline to one that was attainable, even enjoyable. The assistance and support from colleagues in the National Museums and Galleries of Northern Ireland was especially appreciated: in the History Department, colleagues and former colleagues Pauline Dickson, Robert Heslip, Jane Leonard, Bill Maguire and Tom Wylie. Elsewhere in the History Division, we benefited from the interest and encouragement of Cormac Bourke, Winifred Glover, Sinéad McCartan, Jackie Hagan and Richard Warner.

The contributions of our colleagues in the Photographic Departments in both the Ulster Museum and in the Ulster Folk & Transport Museum – Ken Anderson, Alan McCartney, Michael McKeown, Bill Porter, Bryan Rutledge and George Wright – were, if anything, even more heroic than they have been for our previous publications. We should also acknowledge the cooperation of Ulster Museum colleagues in the Marketing Department – Michelle Brady, Pat McLean and Paula Talbot – and in the Art Department – Martyn Anglesea and Elizabeth McCrum – and thank Linda Ballard and the Managing Director, John Wilson, for their support. In the Ulster Folk & Transport Museum Library, information from Roger Dixon and Sally Skilling contributed usefully to our research.

Elsewhere, the help, advice and information courteously provided by the Archivists of Belfast City Council, Robert Corbett, Ian Montgomery and Joseph Heaney, Walter McAuley of the *Belfast Telegraph*, Mark Lenaghan of St Malachy's College and Michael Ridley of the Royal Belfast Academical Institution proved to be very helpful.

This involvement does not, of course, apply to responsibility for any errors or omissions that may be identified and on which the authors would be pleased to receive further information.

All the images reproduced here are from MAGNI's rich and varied collections of historical photographs and the photographic archive.

The authors are pleased to have this opportunity to thank all those individuals who over the years have contributed so generously to the sum of these collections and the archive and to our understanding of them. Readers may also like to know that the collections may be consulted, by appointment with either the Department of History at the Ulster Museum or the Department of Archival Collections (Photography) at the Ulster Folk & Transport Museum.